MARE'S NEST

# MARE'S NEST

## HOLLY MITCHELL

SARABANDE BOOKS  *Louisville, Kentucky*

Publisher's Cataloging-in-Publication Data
(Cassidy Cataloguing Services, Inc.)


Names: Mitchell, Holly, author.
Title: Mare's nest / Holly Mitchell.
Description: First edition. | Louisville, KY : Sarabande Books, [2023]
Identifiers: ISBN: 978-1-956046-12-0 (paperback) | 978-1-956046-13-7 (ebook)
Subjects: LCSH: Families--Poetry. | Coming of age--Poetry. | Horses--Poetry. | Nature--
Poetry. | Fortitude--Poetry. | Fragility (Psychology)--Poetry. | LCGFT: Poetry.
Classification: LCC: PS3613.I8547 M37 2023 | DDC: 811/.6--dc23


Cover design by Sarah Flood-Baumann.
Interior design by Danika Isdahl.
Printed in the USA.
This book is printed on recycled, acid-free paper.

Sarabande Books is a nonprofit literary organization.

The Kentucky Arts Council, the state arts agency, supports Sarabande
Books with state tax dollars and federal funding from the National
Endowment for the Arts.

# CONTENTS

## II.

# MARE'S NEST

# FAMILY NAMES

Pip, *sibling*

Ruth, *maternal grandmother*
Grizzle, *her mother*

Papa, *maternal grandfather*
Paul Weaver (Great-Grandpa Weaver), *his father*
Zennie Weaver (Great-Grandma Weaver, or Grandma),
    *his mother*

Patricia Gail, *maternal aunt*
Teresa Marie, *maternal aunt*
Cheryl, *maternal cousin*

Nana, *paternal grandmother*

**I.**

# MUYBRIDGE'S HORSE IN MOTION

I.

After the beginning of the gallop, there are counts when the horse is in the air, her legs withdrawn, a diamond shape.

This is called suspension.

2.

Her name is Sallie Gardner.

She's by Vandal, out of Charlotte Thompson, Kentucky bred, of Irish pedigree, a Birdcatcher.

Now she belongs to the patron, gold rush tycoon Leland Stanford, who wants to see her in slow motion, to prove a point.

3.

There's more than one way to bet on a racehorse.

A pot maker etches terra cotta, giving the animal wings.

Another artist paints one hoof on the ground.

4.

The camera can make a fool of a realist.

5.

The English photographer has changed his name, returning to the Anglo-Saxon.

*Eadweard Muybridge* will be misspelled on his gravestone.

6.

As *Maybridge*, may the bridge break.

Eadweard's head is hit in a stagecoach crash.

In the Philip Glass score for *The Photographer*, this might be when the staccato starts.

7.

His wife is Flora Shallcross Stone.

When they marry, she's twenty-one, already a divorcée.

Her lover is a theater critic.

That she writes to him shouldn't be fatal.

8.

The photographer shoots the other man who could've fathered their son.

He pleads insanity but gets off on justifiable homicide.

He turns to wet-plate collodion.

9.

After the acquittal, he captures *Sallie Gardner at a Gallop* in twelve frames.

10.

He will live to age seventy-four.

He'll photograph bison, waltzes, and the American West. He'll want an homage to the Great Lakes for his garden.

Then he'll die with prostate cancer while digging a pond.

11.

The child is Florado Helios Muybridge. After the mother wastes away, Eadweard sends the boy to a Catholic orphanage.

For him, this means, instead of encyclopedias, the obscurity of genealogy sites. More is known about the horse.

12.

Sallie is the balanced chestnut of Leland the baron robber from New York.

Even her jockey is a forger.

Sallie's made to run on the private Palo Alto track, tugging the shutters with thread.

The lines are called tripwires.

The cameras in wooden boxes, at last, electric.

# NIGHTMARE

The animal burdened
is cribbing on
a dank fence line.
She appears almost
elegant, ewe-necked
but fescue-footed,
when to the ground
& the meat of
her gored hooves
you inevitably look.
A militant horse
might fight & hasten
the breaking of joints,
yet this mare has
no kick. She looms
over lambkill, the moon
of her moon blindness
near opal, peering quietly
as the ring of ringbone.
That sound is her surra,
a ragged, swaybacked
way of telling you
she is still here
despite the stable flies
stuck on her hide
like beads unshaken
by vertigo. If you lean
close, you can hear
the undertone
of the warble fly

nested under skin,
making a whistler
of the riding horse
now so wind-broken
her breath is kept
in exile, heaving
as she mows this yard
in zodiacal light.

# AFTERBIRTH

(Red bag) my father calls
(placenta pulled over the foal's mouth)

       There are never enough minutes
       to dial the vet

This time my father is alone
rends (it) open with his hands

(Gore veil)

(Inside out first)

(Devil's tear duct)

       *

We boarded broodmares
behind a vineyard

(The grass fescue)

That spring we lost the most

       In a record year
       for (tent worms)

       (Speculated toxins)

\*

My mother pulled (the first)

(The filly) large
through the shoulders
& Mom twisting (her)

      No—
      (the stillborn)

(a face) projecting
from the mare

My mother & father
unsheathed (her)

      Then

I rode to the equine morgue
with (the corpse) under a tarp
in the bed of Dad's pickup

      \*

The mare (survived)
but jumped into barbed wire
(the next day) scarring her chest

      She'd never foal (again)

*

(Flying Nelly)
we nearly watched

(her) slump over
followed by the push
of Wisp's mouth

A red bay colt
to a (red bay dam)

    Soon he bruised himself
    so we nursed (his mother)

    holding her milk
    above his head in IV bags

    ache settling into our arms like praise

*

When (bag) slops
from the mare after birth

we bundle it in empty
feed sacks & twine

We unfold (the map)
looking for tears

(The moonlit sacs
like dragon eyes)

It must be complete

    (The blood) heavily
    attracting coyotes

we lock (the weight of this life)
in Thursday's garbage

    my guard dog trying
    to gobble it down

# GATES IN THE WIND

At night, the husband typed stories.

And the wife played scales on her Western concert flute, tapping out the steps of a march.

Their indoor dogs howled with the chorus, how they used to howl at sirens.

Their outdoor dogs barked deeper than coyotes, forging a field of sound, chasing deer from the pasture.

The neighbors' trucks slowed in the gravel.

But the ATVs rattled on, loud enough to clear a path.

And the horses shuddered awake to run again.

In spring, the broodmares pawed at the plank fences, teasing the alpha female or herdmates' sons, those old enough to be lunged in the far paddock with the one-ton lock.

Then when summer came, fireworks whined, cracked open.

Bullfrogs flung their elastic baritones from the pond to the house.

Cicadas shook the trees after seventeen years underground.

In a thunderstorm, tree limbs slapped the metal roof.

The feet of domestic turkeys scuttled across the porch, scratched on the concrete walkway. All fowl clucked & crooned but only the roosters crowed for an afternoon fight.

It wasn't a hive mind.

Each spoke its own note.

Except for the guinea birds. When they tried to voice their worries, all that came out was the creaking of hinges.

# TURNING OUT (THE FIRST YEAR)

We farm hands move
the mares with foals,
pulling them by halter
to the back paddock.
The dams have waited out
labor & stall rest
for this opening. They paced
in the barn's smallnesses
for months. They crave more
tender grass & sisterhood.
Their foals know just milk
& trying to keep pace.
The herd watches. They are
broodmares too but barren
this year, maybe all years.
They're the too old
& too young. They wait
until someone shows them
what to do. At dusk,
the cool air picks up
hair on everyone's legs.
The hands open the gate.
The mothers canter
& their foals learn the steps
almost in the same motion.
This is turnout.
From the herd, the new
alpha steps forward.
She blocks them with her body,

sixteen hands tall, built
for running distance. She hasn't
given birth or let go
of her sense of order yet.
Through the field, she chases
mares she once knew,
foals she has smelled
but never been permitted
to touch. She almost clips
some flesh in her stride,
almost corners the others
in tines of wire fence.
The mothers rear up.
Behind their shaking legs,
the young narrow themselves.
It isn't natural.
Our family running
to catch a horse by the slips
of leather on her moving face.
It doesn't work. All this
is animal. They spook &
maybe bruise until
tired. The herd splits
for good, hundreds of teeth
snapping on two sides
of the warped fence.

# SEPARATIONS

a barn made for egos
        forbids artificial insemination—

so we load a mare
        every mare
                who's new
                or empty
                or away from her foal—

        we lead her
        by a twitch
                a sedative rope
                gripping her snout—

                maybe she escapes
        with the lead line
trailing under her belly
        as she gallops—

                maybe her foal
                calls for her


                (          )


this is how
        it's done


                my father yells
        then drives
                to the stud farm

        & instead of paying

promises a cut

at auction

      foal share

      or mare share—


I've never watched

      from the viewing box


          above the handlers

          & the rubber floor

          the stallion who

      may or may not know

what to do—


        days after breeding

      the vet palps the mare

      by arm's length


*ever since I left*

        *the womb* he jokes

*I've been trying*

        *to go back—*


a shadow

      on his monitor

her pregnancy

      could be twins

          one to be pinched

             for the other's health


        an abortion

          that Southern men

          think nothing of—

her egg might not stick
could resorb
    before spring

        some mares stay in foal
      through the seasons
          while others just look
            so round
        in their winter coats

# THE BLOOD BAY

*i. The Mother*

holy my father
my brute    my protector
holy their regime

holy my young ones
the smell of them    the noise
of a squalling infancy

holy my old clothes
my breast    my deep
fields of sorrel

holy the foxholes
the howl & dig        the jackdaw
noise & noise holy

the gutted bass    the placement
the naked particulars
my years of pardon


*ii. The Brooddam*

My milk grows
calcium anklets
on the living bones

of my yearlings.
You can't sell them,
so they stay

here in the timothy,
fit only to breed
& fight breeding

each spring. My colostrum
shines on a new mouth.
Our unworded calls

throb through the ground,
unafraid of the coyotes'
duskful peal.

# HAZARD SIGN

on the mauve
of a mare's tongue
taking Regu-Mate
with cracked corn

on the investment
of progesterone effect
to keep her from losing
the ultrasound's blot

to begin her name
with brood- again
to suppress estrus
close the cervix

to prevent twins
among other events
a gambit mimicking
the end of heat

to fool one egg
into sticking
on her thousand pounds
wrapping a uterus

on the hazard sign
the brown plastic bottle
stowed in the fridge
with a broad syringe

# GLOSA ON REBIRTH

*Whose herds with milk, whose fields with bread,*
    *Whose flocks supply him with attire,*
  *Whose trees in summer yield him shade,*
      *In winter fire.*

—Alexander Pope, "Ode on Solitude"

Once I buried myself in a mare's grave.
    But my dog dug up my bones & howled
as if my skeleton were another lost calf
    whose herds with milk, whose fields with bread

whisper for Kentucky's humidity to drop.
    I did not care for times of day or seasons.
Did not want the work of a shepherd
    whose flocks supply him with attire.

My mountain dog led me to the river.
    Dirt falling from my jaw, we walked
through the ashen acres of the deer hunter,
    whose trees in summer yield him shade.

At the riverbank, I held on to exposed roots,
    washing what was left of myself, obedient
as a leaning branch. I kissed the mud until it roused
    & pulsed within my ribs in winter fire.

# KENTUCKY RIVER PALISADES

On the way,
innocuous fruit

interrupts the footpath
lined by black locust—

Osage oranges, Dad says,
of their open pale brains.

Our large white mutt
lopes ahead of us.

After a while,
I think

you'd be dear
to whomever walked with you.

With the current below us,
part of the river

falls over a rockface,
then the exposed banks

with scaffolding
of tangled tree roots

close to death. Opposite,
a tobacco barn

shelters gnats
& rots back into the earth.

Our neighbor's land—
we come down here

on foggy days
when they're not hunting,

but we wear bright colors
just in case—

# FOR MY MOTHER, BAKING RHUBARB

You call me
bunny
You pour the wine

You bury
your never-Village
in the snows I am

crowned
your buttermilk
youngling first

to the scene
Pulling a foal with you
the chestnut lives

Him I towel dry
I remember
the other

first
filly dead in your lap
I accept the

substitution
your *hedge apple* & *keets*
your *handbells*

& *red bag*
for hard fruit
guinea fowl

or showing

      placenta

before mouth

# BW 45MM, 1996

Squatting barefoot on the damp earth,
my mother washes a watermelon
in her favorite water. As it spouts
from Great-Grandma Weaver's creek,
the current runs into a dam made by her uncles,
flows through PVC pipe, carries on—

She is slightly older than me now,
both of her children in another frame.
She smiles & is, her word, skinny
inside one of my father's black T-shirts;
he must be the one taking the picture,
flirting with his first nice camera.

Behind them, the corner of Grandma's house—
where the cornbread cooked,
the biscuits, green beans we'd stripped,
minced ham, canned brown beans—
I wish I could call the food wonderful,
but it is filling as a holiday.

While the photo is taken, I play
on the linoleum floor with Pip,
battling spools & dead ladybugs.
The Greats laugh about our toys,
though they claim it's better for us,
for the generation, not to pop in a VHS.

We're shoeboxes of knickknacks,
the A-frame house everyone fits into.

We're saved, their word, though
we didn't choose to wade out
into a river like they all did.
We're sinners, babies, the best—

We are not yet bodied as Mom,
one to grow larger than her
& the other smaller while she diets.
She cuts the melon that Papa bought
& smiles, already drinking a cup of creek
water, which we say is sweet & clean.

# VULGAR PHASE

Three generations of women
shelled the green beans
we'd eat, pulling the strings
like ripcords, tossing them
in a Homer bucket,

but I slipped away for a taste
of creek water. With Pip,
I uncovered indigo
from loam, a salamander
to read our palms
like a witch making coin.

Listening for a fortune,
we followed sounds
from an unlocked hideout
where we found a TV
& kittens in a hamper.

We broke & entered
as if we hadn't seen
a place so small before.
It was a cousin's trailer.
But that didn't click until
I told our story at dinner

& Mom hissed my name,
*Holly*, like its sly ending
could've lit a stove,
stewing Vidalia onions
with gravel instead of beans.

# WHEN WE MOVED TO THE COUNTRY

You told me you were afraid
        of the silent hickories

& I knew not to punch you
        like when we were small.

But I chose
        a nickname, a girlish

putdown that meant
        I was born first.

I called you Pipsqueak
        when you sang aloud,

shortened to Pip
        when you were sullen

& when you flew
        around the compost pile

you were Pippenbird
        released from farmland.

Now you wear my epithets
        like a dandelion garland,

carry them through fields
        as a hemlock spear.

# THE GOSLING

I found him beside the compost.
Its heat must've hatched him.
His mother was gone, probably
scared off by our parents' trucks.
I asked Pip for a shoebox
we filled with grass blades
& cracked corn, which seemed
like enough. We had just moved
for the acreage. I still slept
on an inflatable inside a bed frame,
drifting off to Bright Eyes
& the Thermals' scratchy music.
The gosling cooed in his box.
Then he died in it within the week
& we buried him, breaking in the land
yards from where the bird began.

# WISP, PEREGRINE


Two or three names we gave him.
When he didn't sell,
my father moved him to a holding pen,
a plank maze
that once led cattle in single file
to food or sex or slaughter.
The question of which kept them walking.
We knocked down some boards,
but there was almost no room for him
to do more than pace,
snap his teeth & get hard
between fence feedings
& piles of hay.
One afternoon, our colt-stallion
zeroed through his gate
into the mares' pasture. He ran
& fucked like a wild animal would not,
taking the pregnant mares in the summer,
through their sutures.
Bella, Star, Put the Heat On—
we could see a blur from the house.
My father caught him with a lead line
& every other bad word he knew.
He sent him up to Mennonites
in Ohio, to be broken
& sold as a different kind of horse—
riding or show? A lie
misted the field, snagged on the fence
& the purplish flowering nettles.

My father told the boarder nothing:
*The girls got awful riled up*
*in that last storm.*

# TETHER

Some evenings
        Dad lashed
the last horse
        who wouldn't budge,
leaving hardly a welt
        with lunge rope
& his muck boots.
        Summer hours
he cooled to stillness
        before dark
& let Mom or me go
        coax the straggler
the slow way
        from aisle to field.
I learned to hand-lead
        from a ripe halter
or a shoulder slick
        with fear. I saw
the glass pupil
        of a racehorse spent,
no, repurposed.
        I read that gender
is our walk.
        Still, animals
find some meaning
        in the movements
we make & keep
        making for them.

## FOALING

I run through the stillbirths—
my father with placenta in his hands.
Over gravel & orchard grass, I run,
the afternoon whipping
my lungs. I reach the
barn with an empty mind.
The young mare bracing,
Mom & I hunch behind her
to pull. We eye & angle
the foal pushed out
in minutes. He breathes.
His mother sighs until she turns
to lick his face dry.
I towel his slick coat.
Mom ties the hanging
afterbirth with twine. We wait
for this knot to pass.
We wait for the colt to stand
& not fall down, to nurse his dam's
nipple after he's tried my thumb.

# NIGHT BREAD

After we feed
the pregnant horses,
Dad works on
the bread maker.

His loaf turns
background music
well into the night.
Pip & I rise,

pausing our movie
to hang about
the kitchen bar.
We break

the crumbling
first slice
of half wheat
with cold butter

& it becomes
possible to
begin to think
of the next.

# WHITE-TAILED FAWN

This time, my father
        waits on the porch
while I'm out driving.

He holds a fawn
        whose neck is broken;
he doesn't know

about the break,
        how the dying will take
an unusual-to-us,

diffuse shape
        like an hourglass
shattered underfoot.

Trying to nurse
        the animal, he offers
a bottle of the milk

he can make without leaving—
        water sweetened
with honey at the tip.

II.

# WEAVER

*An erasure of my great-great-grandfather's obituary*


Spread over a *Blue Back Speller*


He purchased a farm
        married & was considered
                a small country

He held statistics

It is believed he performed
        more than any pastor

He was meat, grain, fruit, vegetable
        & it was necessary to smoke

The home wood-burning
        connected only by a porch

The room large enough

To curtain off the years
        from the nearby
                wound of falling water

# LUMPKIN COUNTY

Walking, Papa says, *There's thorns on that;*
*step on it with your boot so it can't catch you.*

gardens joined
with tacky mortar
stone porch
extension & terraces
planting beds
greenhouse
birdhouse

chicken run
where Pip & I saw
a rabid raccoon
swaying in the passage
now clear
except for a thin skein
of verdant mold

the red clay
some eat to taste
& pecan trees
with only sour pecans left

*Your grandmother loves watermelons*
*but can't have them with her water pills.*

a skylight in a humid room
condensation dappling
half-body mirrors

Mom's teenage poems
embroidered red
into wall hangings
hung beside two
thumb-sized pictures
of her dead sisters

Mom yelling about
spilled peanut soup
as if her mother
isn't shaking
a resting tremor
on the corduroy couch

where I'm sitting
trying to turn
& face everyone
where they're coming from

# HEN HOUSE

Ruth has to slide her hands
under the hot bellies of hens,
take their eggs sticky with flitter.
Red as their rose combs,
she remembers nervous fat,
what a friend's breast felt like
through a linen dress. Brushing
sweat from her widow's peak,
she latches shut the coop
she slept inside as a girl,
tucked away from Grizzle's
hollering *Rooster* after her.
Eggs drop into the basket
she carries out back
where hen-sisters died,
necks pressed to a tree stump
or wrung like dishrags
against barn doors. She washes
the eggs in cold water, arresting
their pink & yellow amnion.
She lays them into cartons
to cool while their sisters
hang from the rafters.
Squint your eyes—tobacco—
juice spilling to the floor.

# THE LAST PORCH SIT

*Chair*

They're not bedsores if it's not a bed

*Spoon-fed*

I feel dolled
& nightmare about

a piebald suit
of old curtains

*I Dread*

The afterparts

when they'll weep
how good I was

*Undecorated*

I turn the rocker
like a sound
pair of hips

family visits
nearly at home

the hours
dark with paper

# GREAT-GRANDMA WEAVER

I thought Zinnia was her proper name. In my journals up until this, I wrote:
Zinnie, *Z–I* like Zinfandel, a sweetness she wouldn't have tasted.

But the stationery at her wake read Mrs. Zennie Weaver with her Zen-like *All
Things Bright & Beautiful* painted in a two-stitch book.

From her creek, I collected, after my mother, four stones.

I wrote, for my mother, our chicken hearts were cleaned, but they weren't.

The stones were lost in my pockets.

They were not organs.

Zennie who made everything by hand can't tell me what to do with the state.

I'm still turning over words for matriarch. Dame, dowager, matron, queen. Is
money the only way we can name a woman—

Zennie's *E*'s, clay engravery, an endmark cleft.

When I Googled Zennie Weaver, I saw Zennies & Weavers pieced together from
other families until I found my Zennie Weaver of the 1940 US Census, twenty-six
years old, wife of head of household. She checked off white, American, female &
counted four sons of the eventual eight children.

The obituary labels her homemaker instead of subsistence farmer & rattles off her
talents as if to give her away at some downtown cotillion.

When I return to her home in Dahlonega, I take a seed catalog & a softwood swan.

Mom says her cousin Cheryl must've whittled it. Cheryl says, Oh that old thing, I
dunno anymore.

# INVOCATION

I am ashamed to call, Great-Grandpa Weaver,
because I have forgotten where you are buried.

Yet, I call on the tenuous memory of you.
Because I have forgotten where you are buried,

I will wait for whatever voice you send, a rasp
because I have forgotten where you are buried

or a congregation of Paul Weavers singing—
*because I have forgotten where you are buried—*

a Depression of an answer I will accept.
Because I have forgotten where you are buried,

I listen for silent grace. Your corn liquor low
because I have forgotten where you are buried,

I will not burden you with the names I bottle.
Because I have forgotten where you are buried,

I name the oxen Red & their calves Red again
because I have forgotten. Where you are buried,

there's glass . . . at Tickanetley. I can only remember
because I had forgotten where.

# GAINESVILLE

Teresa Marie
& Patricia Gail,
my mother's dead

sisters who stayed blonde.
Honeyed like newspaper
clippings, they are buried

under clay bowls, platitude,
embroidery. As a child,
I found my aunts

in stories of Gainesville
before the constant television
& rock wall behind it,

a birthplace emptied,
daughters driven to Atlanta
or left with beaten dogs & smoke.

That ringing ear told my mother
her sisters were unbaptized dead
& dying: How come you don't

know to wash
the dishes under hot water?
Her Gainesville turned

& pulled away, skipping church
to drive deeper into the Blue
Mountain Chain, taking the body

of wild mushrooms,
the blood of natural springs.
I cannot imagine

my mother in the years
now crystallized
between hospital & house,

mutated cells & vegetable-fruits,
the parents (carriers) who let
buttermilk sour, crushed

mints beneath a yellowbook.
The Gainesville I know
walks in the stone garden

full of nightshades, calling
each day to hear
her voice on the line—

# EARTHBOUND

Where do I go when earthbound—
     a Martian left in the hills?
Some days I drive alone
     with rock weighing down my truck.
Others, I bring my wife,
     a stark human beauty
who doesn't find me strange
     in this Georgia-red skin—
returned from the ships of war
     to lay stone, constellating
gardens, driveways, property lines.
     In the bend where we first kissed
I spot an airship
     so familiar I lose my voice.
When I tell our firstborn,
     my surviving child,
in a whisper, she giggles
     & calls me crazy, twirling
her hair like copper wire.
     Every week, she stays up
to sneak *The Twilight Zone*
     though I hear well
the turning of the dial.

# BOTTLE ROCKETS

*i.*

The sharp smell of light
          burst-broke into the sky

twenty-odd years ago
          on Nana's last Fourth

of July evening
          with all her sons.

And here we are a family
          still afraid to cry

in the quietude
          of our new home

hidden in a pasture
          where horses graze.

At any flash-clap
          the broodmares lose it

jumping fences
          herds & rank until

they limp away
          from their panic

with cattle wire coiled
          behind the hoof wall.

*ii.*
We dress their wounds
    when we are theirs,

working until we are
    raised bruises.

# CARPENTRY

My father built the stalls with his father
changing the word for the barn
from tobacco to horse

I asked to use the scrap
to craft a ramp for my terrier
started with the nails going nowhere
bending under the borrowed hammer

then my father helped with curses
explaining the wood was bad
ready for the burn pile

*

(Dodger didn't understand
        when I placed his paws
on Frankenstein's plank & rungs

I still had to lift him up
        shuttle him down / listen
to his keening / he wouldn't jump

heights on his own
        he waited for me / howled
louder than the future)

*

in my mind / my mountains

I make another / small home

a small home / I spoon pit-labs

I shave my head / a clipper

guard number / I wear the same

box of a jacket / without debt

# AS WE SANG ON CINDER BLOCKS

I wanted everything
               from my friends
& held them
               to mythic standards,
the scaffolding
               of stranded flowers.
I wasn't the villain
                         in my roving, not rovery,
but felt unfair as a crush,
                         mess as an action.
What I'd been told
               of sugar was false.
I thought I wanted
               to be chosen
when I needed to choose
                         the age-old sunrise
unrolling closer,
               warmer than before.

# YOUR BONFIRE

arches into dusk.
A frog reaches out,
her arms flattened in the gravel drive.
            So this is your home.
These are your denim boys,
your video games & honeysuckle,
your burnt meats.
This is your father's
forbidden jug of peach wine,
your grandmother's pair of pit bulls,
your oiled ATV.
The boys I know are leaving
fast in their tinted cars.
Katie unfurls in the hammock, text
messages from Phoenix
landing on her browned lap
like sparks. Another rising
freshman melts into your thigh.
While I fetch tinder,
a strand of your long red hair
flies inside my mouth.
            This means almost nothing
but you can't have it back.

# HORSE THEATER

I am outside watching
a pregnant mare in the field

when an ex visits.
How exciting, he must think

we'll birth a foal together,
but she's just sweating.

I am leaving for the summer.
He asks where

is the place to piss.
We can walk to the house,

but he insists on the barn
where I work. He marks

the straw like a colt would
without thinking yes or no.

I step away as if not
to remember. Approaching

the past-due mare, I brush
dirt from her mane

& clean the serif line
about her eyes.

I put my nose before hers
& breathe in like a horse.

It's bad husbandry.
She could kill me like this,

but she sniffs so readily
as if she couldn't wait to talk.

# PATTI SMITH'S HORSES

The internet sends *Horses*
    Horses then burst

Burst through the windows
    Windows & "Land"

Land inside my ear
    Ear almost catches

Catches in the crescent
    Crescendo of hooves

Hooves half buckled
    Half buckled with water

Water still listening
    Glistening on a record

Record makes a person
    Person not sound alone

Alone in the sunroom
    Sunroom split with light

Light's prism turning
    Turning out horses

*Horses . . . in all directions*
    Directing me on

# THE TORNADO'S WARNING

My old Kentucky,
I am no thorn.
But in my eye, I feel
small & unlikely
to be crossed
more than once. I crumble
murals of dead men
in their colonial
tricorns. I tear up
a road you call an alley
because it dares cut close
to the Sears homes.
I whisper devotions,
spells that don't work,
the music I hum to you
to bring myself down.
After all, my congregation,
it's just dew
oracular on the web.
This morning, a spider
patched it as if for the sole
purpose of meeting
its fragile glamour
with mine, gray
from birth. What
on earth did I mean
by appearing? I will
let you parse that.
Onto the next state

I rope out, wider,
though no less precise.
I hear the infinite
was created before
the finite. I take
only what can be swept—
the paper in the branches
of a black locust, the borer
bored inside the tree's trunk,
wrapped with my prize,
the ashen crown of spires
I've come back to collect.

# I HOPE I DIDN'T WRITE A SOUTH WHERE NO ONE

is dieting or crash dieting
        or takes shots of seaweed
or has allergies
      to nonallergenic foods
or talks about pie
      instead of queerness

or looks at domestic fowl
       & plans a meal when
no one owns a turkey fryer
       grills in the driveway
or attends beef festivals
      or beer cheese fairs

where no one binges
      chess or potato pie
& no one bourbon
     never hugging
       the porcelain like
no one cooks in Coke
     or Sprite & sugar
feeding in place of saying
      I saw your receipts

no one insists
    on Pizza Fridays
       instead of phone calls
Nacho Thursdays
    instead of therapy
& no local rises
    to the next level

of stupidity denying
                    the beauty of tallow


no one suffers
                    tortilla chip fissures
or drinks their red
                    wine cold from the box
keeps peppered ham
                    in the second freezer
or on a dry Derby Day
                    cubes summer sausage
or venison hunted
                    behind the property


where no one serves children
                    the squirrel bacon
from their troop mates'
                    first BB gun kills
or shares maternal stories
                    of boar roast
& being tricked
                    to eat horse meat


washed down with
                    instant lemonade
from a plastic pitcher
                    clear with a blue lid
no one blends
                    the lemonade with buttermilk
or finds themselves
                    dining on trouble
                                        just because
a mother boiled it
                    in her second-best pot

# ACKNOWLEDGMENTS

I am grateful to the editors who first chose poems from this collection for the following publications:

"Muybridge's Horse in Motion," *Narrative*
"Turning Out (The First Year)," *The Baltimore Review*
"Separations," *LIBER: A Feminist Review*
"Glosa on Rebirth," *The Oxonian Review*
"Kentucky River Palisades," *Office Hours Broadside Exhibition*, with visual art
      by Lee Maxey
"For My Mother, Baking Rhubarb" (previously titled "Rhubarb Fool"), *Paperbag*
"Hen House" and "The Last Porch Sit," *Steaming*
"Your Bonfire," *SPLIT Quarterly*
"Patti Smith's Horses," *Afternoon Visitor*
"The Tornado's Warning" (previously titled "Tornado Warning), *Day One*
"I Hope I Didn't Write a South Where No One," *No, Dear*

Thank you to Sarah Gorham for believing in my manuscript and editing it with boldness and clarity, and to the Sarabande Books team—Sam Hall, Kristen Renee Miller, Danika Isdahl, Joanna Englert, and Natalie Wollenzien, and also Jordan Koluch.

Thanks to those who read this manuscript at any stage: Emily Wallis Hughes, Shamar Hill, Darren Bowman, Stephanie Jean, Abdul Ali, and Sarah Sala in recent years;

Bianca Lynne Spriggs, Alicia Rebecca Myers, Nigel Alderman, Robert B. Shaw, and Roger Babb in the early days; and Yusef Komunyakaa, who read it back to me. Deep gratitude for my teachers Aracelis Girmay, Sara London, Cynthia Cruz, Catherine Barnett, Matthew Rohrer, Terrance Hayes, and Edward Hirsch. I owe much to my brilliant cohort from New York University's Creative Writing Program and to the Office Hours Poetry Workshop, especially Sophia Holtz, JJ Starr, Alexandria Hall, Francisco Márquez, Mal Profeta, Laura Cresté, Linda Harris Dolan, Victoria Sanz, Vanessa Moody, Caitlin McDonnell, Jen Levitt, and Marty Correia.

I am forever indebted to the Kentucky Governor's School for the Arts, to my teachers—Ellen Hagan, Crystal Wilkinson, Kelly Norman Ellis, and Dan Bernitt—who inspired me to write into adulthood, and to the girls who turned being a teen poet into a strength. I also want to name Nickole Brown and Nikky Finney and the institutions and groups that made ongoing poetry workshops and readings accessible to me: the Carnegie Center for Literacy and Learning, the Kentucky Women Writers Conference, the Affrilachian Poets, The Twenty: Young Writers Advance, and Hindman Settlement School.

My family, I am grateful for your encouragement and support. Thank you, Vivian, for your generosity and unflagging confidence in my work. My dear Suzette, you made this and the rest possible with love.

# LEXICON

*Bay*—a dark coat, brown to reddish brown.

*Blood bay*—an auburn coat.

*Brooddam*—a broodmare.

*Broodmare*—a female horse kept for breeding foals.

*Chestnut*—a light, coppery coat.

*Colt*—a young male horse.

*Dam*—a horse who is a mother.

*Estrus* is heat, or the part of the female sexual reproductive cycle just prior to ovulation.

*Ewe-necked* describes a genetic deformity that causes a U-shaped depression in a horse's neck.

*Fescue-footed* refers to lameness, or inability to walk properly, caused by ingesting a fungus that lives on mature fescue grass.

*Filly*—a young female horse.

*Foal*—a baby horse.

*Glosa* is a poetic form in which the lines of the poem's epigraph are repeated in order as the last line of each stanza of the poem.

*Homer bucket* is the name for a standard-issue plastic bucket with a wire handle.

*Keets* are baby guinea fowl.

*Lambkill*, or sheep laurel, is a poisonous plant.

*Lunge*—to exercise a horse on a lunge line by having it run in a circle around the trainer.

*Mare*—a mature female horse.

*Mare's nest* is idiomatic for "a complex and difficult situation; a muddle" and "an illusory discovery" (Oxford English Dictionary online, 2022).

*Moon blindness* results from a bacterial eye infection.

Muybridge's *The Horse in Motion* is an early photo experiment that proved horses lift off into the air at full run (gallop).

*Pinch*—a veterinary abortion.

*Red bag* refers to when the placenta presents first in a birth.

*Red bay*—an auburn coat.

*Regu-Mate* is synthetic progesterone used to suppress ovulation and reduce the risk of miscarriage in a broodmare.

*Ringbone* is new bone growth affecting the lower leg.

*Stallion*—a mature male horse that has not been neutered.

*Stud*—a stallion kept for breeding.

*Surra* refers to heavy breathing and a disease transmitted by flies.

*Swaybacked* describes an abnormally curved spine.

*Timothy* is a grass that's safe for horses to eat.

*Twitch*—an old tool made of a wooden handle and rope that helps control a horse by pinching the upper lip.

*Vandal*, *Charlotte Thompson*, and *Birdcatcher* are thoroughbred racehorses in Sallie Gardner's pedigree.

*Whistler*—a horse with a permanent wheeze.

*Wind-broken* refers to that wheeze.

*Yearling*—a one-year-old horse.

**HOLLY MITCHELL** is a poet from Kentucky, now based in New York. A winner of an Amy Award from Poets & Writers, Holly received an MFA in Creative Writing from New York University and a BA in English from Mount Holyoke College. Holly's poems have appeared or are forthcoming in *Steaming* (an online publication by *Fence*), *Afternoon Visitor*, and the *Lambda Literary Poetry Spotlight*, among other journals.

Sarabande Books is a nonprofit literary press located in Louisville, KY. Founded in 1994 to champion poetry, short fiction, and essay, we are committed to creating lasting editions that honor exceptional writing. For more information, please visit sarabandebooks.org.